JOHN *Adams*

John *Adams*

OUR SECOND PRESIDENT

By Ann Graham Gaines

SPIRIT
of America™

The Child's World®, Inc.
Chanhassen, Minnesota

7

JOHN *Adams*

Published in the United States of America by The Child's World®, Inc.
PO Box 326 • Chanhassen, MN 55317-0326 • 800-599-READ • www.childsworld.com

Acknowledgments
The Creative Spark: Mary Francis-DeMarois, Project Director; Elizabeth Sirimarco Budd, Series Editor; Robert Court, Design and Art Direction; Janine Graham, Page Layout; Jennifer Moyers, Production

The Child's World®, Inc.: Mary Berendes, Publishing Director; Red Line Editorial, Fact Research; Cindy Klingel, Curriculum Advisor; Robert Noyed, Historical Advisor

Photos
Cover: White House Collection, courtesy White House Historical Association; Courtesy of the Adams National Historical Park: 7, 15, 21, 31, 34 (left); Corbis: 24, 32; Independence National Historical Park: 16, 17, 18, 20; The Library of Congress Collection: 9, 12, 13, 19, 27, 28, 30; Courtesy of the Massachusetts Historical Society: 6, 10, 14, 35; Stock Montage: 26, 29; White House Collection, courtesy White House Historical Association: 34 (right)

Registration
The Child's World®, Inc., Spirit of America™, and their associated logos are the sole property and registered trademarks of The Child's World®, Inc.

Library of Congress Cataloging-in-Publication Data
Gaines, Ann.
    John Adams : our second president / Ann Graham Gaines.
        p. cm.
    Includes bibliographical references and index.
    ISBN 1-56766-843-7 (alk. paper)
    1. Adams, John, 1735–1826—Juvenile literature. 2. Presidents—United States—
Biography—Juvenile literature. [1. Adams, John, 1735–1826. 2. Presidents.] I. Title.
    E322 .G19 2000
    973.4'4'092—dc21

00-011354

14   21   26

Contents

Chapter ONE

American Patriot

John Adams was a young, newly married lawyer when Benjamin Blyth painted this portrait in 1764. Both Adams's parents had hoped that he would one day become a minister, but he chose to study law instead.

JOHN ADAMS, THE SECOND PRESIDENT OF THE United States, was a very important leader in the American Revolution. He remained one of the new nation's great thinkers. Even so, he is not remembered as a great president. But Adams would have argued that he made a valuable contribution to the country during his presidency. After all, he kept the nation out of a war with France.

John Adams was born on October 30, 1735, in Braintree, Massachusetts (a small town 12 miles from Boston). His parents owned a farm. Their rocky land was hilly, but they managed to raise good crops. Adams's father was an important man in Braintree. He was a church **deacon** and a member of the town council.

Adams's mother and father read all the time. At a young age, John began to love books as well. He knew how to read by the time he went to a school that was similar to kindergarten. He liked it there, but he soon got old enough to go to the town's public school. His new teacher did not pay enough attention to his students. Adams later said this made him dislike going to school. He was happier outside, where he and his two brothers played marbles, wrestled, swam, and skated. He made toy boats to sail and kites to fly.

John Adams was born on his parents' farm, shown in the painting above, in Braintree, Massachusetts. His father's family had lived in Massachusetts for five generations.

7

For a while, John Adams thought he wanted to grow up to become a farmer like his father. He saw no reason to go to college. Then, when he was 14, his father sent him to a school with a better teacher. Adams studied so hard that he was ready to go to Harvard College in just one year. At the time, there were just a few colleges in the American colonies, and Harvard was the best. Going there almost guaranteed success in life. He graduated from Harvard in 1755.

While in college, he had decided to become a lawyer. There were no law schools in those days. Students paid lawyers to **tutor** them in their offices. Adams moved to the town of Worcester to become a teacher. He used the money he earned to pay his tutor.

Adams made many friends. A deep thinker as well as an avid reader, he liked to talk about **politics** with them. But other people's ideas rarely **influenced** him. All his life, Adams would have an independent mind.

In 1756, at age 21, Adams had earned enough money to pay for lessons in law. In two years, he opened his own law office in Braintree, and 10 years later moved to Boston, the capital of the colony of Massachusetts.

8

Boston was a big town on a harbor, which was always filled with ships. Adams was amazed by how busy it was. Its streets were filled with "Chimney Sweeps, Carriers of Wood, Merchants, Ladies, Priests, Carts, Horses, Oxen, Coaches, Market men and women, Soldiers, Sailors." There was so much noise, sometimes it was difficult to think.

As a lawyer, his work took him to courts all over Massachusetts. He earned a reputation for being smart and for winning arguments. He also became known for his quick temper.

Harvard College was established in 1636. Today known as Harvard University, it is the oldest college in the United States. When John Adams entered Harvard in 1751, he became the first in his family to go to college.

John Adams adored his intelligent and kind wife, Abigail. They had a wonderful marriage, and he called her his best friend. "Miss Adorable," he once wrote to her, "I hereby order you to give [me] as many kisses, and as many hours of your company … as [I] shall please to demand."

In 1761, Adams's father died, leaving him a house in Braintree as an **inheritance.** In 1764, John Adams married Abigail Smith. They moved to Braintree to start their family. Over the years, Adams became more interested in politics. He began to write articles and books on the subject. People read everything he wrote. He became a **spokesperson** for the patriots, the colonists who thought the colonies should break away from England.

England had begun to pass laws that said colonists had to pay taxes. English **officials** collected these taxes from the colonists and sent them to the king of England. In 1770 and 1771, John Adams was elected to the Massachusetts **legislature.** For a long time, he hoped the patriots would not have to fight to win independence for the colonies. But in December of 1773, colonists protested new taxes placed on tea at the Boston Tea Party. They disguised themselves as Indians and boarded British ships carrying tea that had docked in Boston's harbor. Then they dumped all the tea into the water. It was ruined and could not be sold. England would earn no taxes from it. Adams described it as "the grandest event which has ever yet happened."

The angry British government closed the harbor at Boston, letting no ships sail in or out. This left the town short of supplies, which Adams thought was unfair. He became convinced a **revolution** was coming. He committed himself to joining the patriots, saying he would "live or die, survive or perish with my country."

In 1774, John Adams was elected to the First **Continental Congress.** He closed his law office to enter politics. The colonists thought he did a very good job, so they elected him to the Second Continental Congress as well. The colonies declared their independence in 1776, and the United States was born.

In 1777, Congress asked John Adams to become a **diplomat** to Holland and France. The new country needed **representatives** to go to Europe to meet with officials from other countries. He was amazed by what he saw there, admiring the beautiful palaces, paintings,

▶ Late in his life, John Adams claimed that many of the ideas in the Declaration of Independence were his, although Thomas Jefferson actually wrote it. One draft by Jefferson does have comments scribbled in by Adams.

and sculptures in the grand cities of Europe. But he would always think Americans had a better life. Throughout the 10 years he worked as a diplomat, he looked forward to going home. He especially missed his family. Abigail and their children still lived in Braintree, where they tended the family farm.

Benjamin Franklin, John Adams, and Thomas Jefferson (from left to right) were all on the committee that Congress charged with writing the Declaration of Independence. Although Jefferson actually wrote this important document, Adams and Franklin gave him advice and support.

ON MARCH 5, 1770, British soldiers fired into a crowd and killed five colonists in Boston. Samuel Adams, John Adams's cousin, immediately called the event the "Boston Massacre." He asked Paul Revere to create a picture of it, and copies were sent all over the colonies.

Revere's picture is shown above. Learning about the Boston Massacre stirred up patriotic feelings among the colonists.

John Adams, however, believed that both the British and the Americans were to blame for the massacre. He considered the deaths tragic, but he also thought the American mob had behaved badly. As a lawyer, he even defended the British soldiers in court. All but two of these soldiers were found innocent. This is an example of what an independent thinker Adams was. He was a patriot, yet he helped the English soldiers who he thought were being treated unfairly.

Chapter TWO

A Weak Vice President

Adams twice went to Holland, asking leaders there to lend money to the United States. A Dutch artist made this portrait of him during his time there.

JOHN ADAMS WAS A GOOD DIPLOMAT. He worked hard explaining to European kings and officials why Americans wanted and deserved their independence. In 1778, he helped convince France to fight with the United States in the Revolution, which greatly strengthened American forces. In 1780, he convinced Holland to lend the United States money and to recognize its independence.

The British general, Charles Cornwallis, **surrendered** to General George Washington in 1781, and the American Revolution ended. It took two more years for the United States and England to sign a peace **treaty.** John Adams, Benjamin Franklin, and John Jay were the Americans who **negotiated** it. Then Adams went back to Holland, where he got another loan for his country. Next, Adams moved to London, where he was the first American diplomat recognized by the king of England. Finally, after many years of separation, his wife and daughter came to live with him.

After the Revolution ended, American leaders had time to discuss exactly what form of government the new nation needed. In 1787, a book Adams wrote about **constitutions** was published. Representatives at the **Constitutional Convention** read what Adams had written. His words guided them as they decided what to include in the U.S. Constitution. His ideas helped shape the American government.

John Adams always wanted the new nation to establish a **democracy.** He once wrote that he was a firm "enemy to **monarchy,"** countries such as England that were ruled by a king or queen. In a democracy, citizens have freedom of speech, and Adams worked hard to make sure that Americans could openly express their opinions. On the other hand, a democracy should allow all its citizens the right to vote.

Before Adams left for Europe, he bought this locket for Abigail. It features a painting of a woman gazing sadly at a ship headed out to sea. Adams thought it would symbolize the pain his wife felt at his departure.

Adams did not think that everyone should have that right. He believed only people with money and education should be allowed to vote. Adams paid close attention as the Constitutional Convention determined such matters, although he was still thousands of miles away in England.

In 1788, John Adams and his family returned to the United States. Crowds turned out to meet them. The Massachusetts legislature sent him an official notice saying how pleased the colony was to have Adams and his family safely back in Massachusetts. It also recognized his hard work.

16

He retired to Braintree to farm, but a year later, he agreed to run in the first presidential election ever held in the United States. The **electoral college** cast the most votes for George Washington. John Adams came in second, which in the early years of the nation meant he became the vice president.

Although his election excited him at first, Adams did not like his new job. George Washington did not consider Adams his assistant. He believed the vice president's job was simply to **preside** over the Senate. So Adams attended and ran Senate sessions. If any vote ended in a tie, it was his job to cast the tie-breaking vote. Although he was not a senator, he voted to break a tie 20 times when the senators could not agree on whether a **bill** should become law. This did not satisfy him. A smart man who was used to having people listen to him, Adams was unhappy. Sometimes he became angry when people did not share his point of view. He thought people were fools to disagree with him. Adams complained that the vice presidency was "the most insignificant office" that any person had ever held.

John Adams was never very happy as George Washington's vice president. Nevertheless, he and Abigail always felt great affection and respect for both George and Martha Washington. In fact, they regarded them so highly that Adams had these portraits painted and then hung them in his family's dining room.

17

▸ When John Adams was a diplomat in Europe, he made many important decisions without consulting U.S. leaders. To ask Congress what to do would have taken too long. It took many weeks for a letter and its response to go back and forth across the ocean.

▸ John Adams administered the oath of office to George Washington at his **inauguration** on April 30, 1789.

Both Adams and Abigail experienced great unhappiness during this time. At first, she lived with him in New York, the capital city at the time. But she later went back to live in Quincy (Braintree's new name). She and John had found it too expensive to live in New York because they were expected to have many parties with expensive food and wine. They missed each other terribly, but John Adams believed he still had a duty to serve the nation. He agreed to a second term as vice president.

In 1796, George Washington refused to run for president a third time. John Adams agreed to run for the office, and he hoped he would be elected. When he was vice president, he once wrote, "I am weary of the game [of politics], yet I don't know how I could live out of it." A proud man, he also believed he would do well. He did not realize how important it is for a president to get along with other people.

Adams described himself during the vice presidency as "a mere mechanical tool to wind up the clock." He was pleased when his time in that office was over.

18

JOHN ADAMS DEPENDED ON HIS wife throughout their 54-year marriage. Born Abigail Smith, she was the daughter of a minister. Hers was a cultured and important family. She had no more education than other women of her day, but she was intelligent and interested in ideas.

When Adams went to Europe as a diplomat, Abigail remained home for a long time. During most of the Revolution, she and their children lived on their farm at Quincy. She supported the family by running the farm. After the war ended, she and their daughter sailed to England to be with John, where she charmed British leaders and made her husband's job much easier. She later played an important public role back in the United States as well.

Today Abigail Adams continues to inspire American women. Devoted to her husband and her family, she also had a very active life of the mind. She was one of the first Americans who spoke about women's rights. She was unhappy that women had few opportunities. For one thing, she believed women had a right to an education. In a famous letter to John Adams, written in March 1776, she told him to "remember the ladies" as he helped craft the **policies** of what would soon be a new nation. "Do not put such unlimited power into the hands of the Husbands," wrote Abigail.

19

Chapter THREE

The Presidency

Politician Alexander Hamilton (above) and John Adams both belonged to the Federalist Party, but they did not get along. Hamilton wanted his ideas to influence the president, but Adams—always an independent thinker— would not listen to him.

BY THE TIME JOHN ADAMS BECAME THE nation's second president, **political parties** had begun to form. Adams, like Washington before him, thought that these groups would make it more difficult for politicians to cooperate and get things done. They would be too busy arguing with people from other political parties who had ideas different from their own.

By the late 1790s, however, politicians needed the support of a party to win an election. So Adams let the **Federalist Party** **nominate** him. The **Republican Party** nominated Thomas Jefferson. When the electoral votes were counted, Adams had received 71, and Jefferson had received 68. Adams had just barely won.

20

This portrait features Adams in the suit he wore to his inauguration. Although his presidency would be a troubled one, Adams managed to keep the new government stable by keeping many of Washington's policies.

John Adams's inauguration took place in 1797. At the ceremony, Washington, who was about to retire, received more attention than Adams, but Adams did not seem to mind. Always a hardworking man, he set to work right after the ceremony. One thing he did not have to do was choose a **cabinet.** He simply kept the cabinet members George

Washington had chosen. This later became a problem. At the end of his presidency, George Washington often took the advice of Alexander Hamilton. Although Hamilton left Washington's cabinet, he still influenced his former coworkers. He was also the leader of the Federalist Party. Unfortunately, Hamilton and Adams disliked each other.

Hamilton expected to influence Adams because they belonged to the same political party. But Adams did not want anyone's advice. He believed that Americans expected the man they elected president to think for himself. This made Hamilton angry. Adams grew angry as well when he began to see that the cabinet was more loyal to Hamilton than to him.

Foreign affairs took up most of Adams's time while he was president. After the American Revolution, England and France both treated the United States poorly. Nearly a decade before, in 1789, a violent revolution had erupted in France. That country's king was replaced with a new government, which declared that France would overthrow other countries' monarchies as well.

Then, in 1793, France declared war on Spain and Great Britain. The French expected Americans to fight with them. Earlier, the United States and France had signed a treaty that said the United States would join France if it ever went to war. Most Americans did not want to keep this promise. In fact, President Washington declared the United States **neutral.**

The creation of the United States led some Europeans to question whether monarchs had a supreme right to rule the people. By 1789, the citizens of France had begun their own revolution.

Many Americans did not want the United States to fight for France. They did not think the French had the right to overthrow other peoples' governments. But some Americans thought the United States owed loyalty to France because it had helped them win the American Revolution.

By the time Adams became president in 1797, the French had decided they wanted nothing to do with the United States. They ordered an American diplomat to leave France. They also stopped trading goods with the United States. At sea, French ships attacked American ships.

In the cartoon, speech banners read:

"Cease bawling, Monster! We will not give you six pence."

"Il faut de l'argent, il faut beaucoup d'argent. Money, Money, Money!!"

CIVIC FEAST

French officials demanded $250,000 before they would even listen to the Americans who had come to fix problems between the two countries. This political cartoon depicts France as a five-headed monster demanding money from the U.S. representatives.

In 1797, Adams sent American officials to talk to the French about these problems. Unfortunately, French leaders refused to see the Americans unless they paid a **bribe.** They also demanded that the American government lend France a huge amount of money. The American officials sent messages to Adams telling him what had happened. In these letters, they referred to the French leaders not by their real names, but by the letters X, Y, and Z.

24

President Adams refused to pay France the money it wanted. He went to Congress to tell his fellow politicians about the "XYZ Affair." Adams asked Congress to get ready to fight the French, but not to actually declare war. The public supported Adams.

In 1798, it looked as if war would soon break out between the United States and France. Adams ordered new ships to be built for the American navy. He asked George Washington to serve as commander in chief of the army. This meant Washington took a position that should be the president's, according to the Constitution. But Adams believed Washington could do a better job.

Many Americans began to fear that foreigners might try to destroy the American government. A French general had already come to North America and tried to set up another new nation to the west of the United States. Many Americans considered this a serious threat.

To keep the United States safe, Congress passed the **Alien** and **Sedition** Acts. There were three Alien Acts, two of which could be used to make foreigners leave the country—even if they

In this 1798 cartoon, the Federalists and Republicans in Congress are shown fighting about the Alien and Sedition Acts. Federalists believed the acts would prevent enemies from hurting the United States. Republicans believed the new laws denied the rights guaranteed by the Constitution.

had done nothing wrong. A third act increased the length of time it took for **immigrants** to become U.S. citizens. The Sedition Act said that no one, whether an American or a foreigner, could say anything bad about the government or its leaders.

Adams had not asked for these acts to be passed. In fact, he did not want them, but he did sign them into law. Some important leaders thought this was a terrible mistake. They pointed out, for one thing, that the Sedition Act took away Americans' freedom of speech. The laws expired in 1801. Today historians agree that the laws were dangerous.

26

TODAY WASHINGTON, D.C., IS THE CAPITAL CITY OF THE UNITED STATES, but it did not even exist when John Adams was elected vice president. First the capital was in New York and later in Philadelphia. Soon government leaders decided to build a brand new capital city. The first public buildings that went up were the Capitol and the president's mansion.

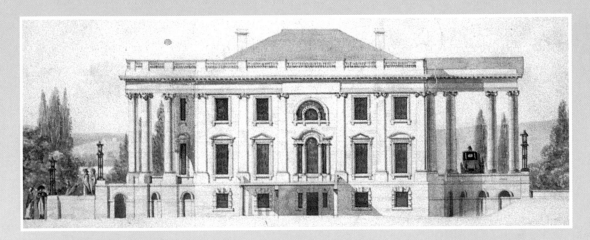

When the Adamses arrived in Washington, D.C., the city was still being built. There were fields and swamps in the center of town. They became the first residents of the president's mansion on November 1, 1800. It wasn't until President James Monroe's term that people would begin calling the mansion the White House.

The president's mansion was very large. Eventually, it would be elegant, too, but it was as yet unfinished. Abigail Adams described it as a castle but noted that it sat amid what was still a wild landscape. She wrote to a friend that she had ridden into town on a dirt path. In town, carriages got stuck in muddy streets, and people had to climb out and walk the rest of the way. When she arrived in the city, there was not yet a library or even a church.

Chapter FOUR

Saving the Nation from War

Throughout his presidency, Adams was concerned with foreign affairs. He hoped to stay out of the war between France and England and believed—just as George Washington had—that the United States should remain neutral.

FROM 1798 TO 1800, AMERICAN VESSELS fought the French in an undeclared war at sea. By this time, Adams began to think his most important job was to work for peace. He found himself practically alone in this opinion, however. Adams was a stubborn man, and he had never learned to compromise. He had failed to form many political friendships. Still, he remained committed to his ideals.

Most of all, Adams wanted the United States to grow and prosper. He was afraid that war would hurt the new country too much, perhaps even causing it to fall apart. He worked on a peace plan all by himself. Finally, he sent a peace mission to France, which succeeded in stopping the battles at sea. This actually turned many Americans—supporters of Alexander

From 1798 through 1800, U.S. ships battled the French navy, although the two nations were never actually at war. President Adams never declared war because he hoped that France would be too busy fighting battles against European nations to concern itself with North America.

Hamilton—against him. They believed the country should have gone to war against France. Adams was accused of being unfit to serve as president. The situation upset him.

Even while under attack, Adams did his job. In 1800, the **federal** government moved to Washington, D.C., the nation's new capital city. John Adams moved into what Americans now call the White House, becoming the first president to live there. Abigail soon arrived, too.

Adams ran for a second term as president but lost the election to Thomas Jefferson. His feelings were hurt. He believed Americans did not understand all he had done for them. Late in his life he wrote, "I never engaged in public affairs for my own interest, pleasure, envy … or even the desire of fame."

Thomas Jefferson (right) and Adams had been close friends during the Revolution, but their opposing ideas separated them as the new nation took shape. The election of 1800 saw Adams and Jefferson running against each other again. But this time, Jefferson would win.

The very day Jefferson was sworn in as the third president of the United States, Adams left Washington. He was glad to return to Quincy. Earlier, he had written to Abigail of his feeling that he would never have a place of his own: "Oh! that I could have a home! But this felicity has never been permitted me."

In Quincy, he enjoyed working on his farm and writing and receiving letters. He read a great deal and enjoyed spending time with his children, grandchildren, and great-grandchildren who lived close to him.

After he lost the election of 1800, John Adams returned to Massachusetts. He and Abigail moved into a house they had purchased 12 years before. The house is known today as "Old House," and it is still in existence.

In 1825, Adam's son, John Quincy Adams, became the president. Like his father, John Quincy Adams had a difficult presidency. After it was over, he described his term of office as "the four most miserable years of my life."

For a long time after retiring, John Adams stayed active. Toward the very end, however, he began to look and feel old. He could no longer see or hear well, but his mind stayed clear.

On October 28, 1818, Abigail Adams died, to her husband's great sorrow. They had been married for 54 years. In 1825, his son, John Quincy Adams, became the sixth president of the United States. The new president immediately sat down and wrote to his father in Quincy. John Adams replied, "The multitude of my thoughts, and the intensity of my feelings are too much." In private, he said to a neighbor, "No man who ever held the office of president would congratulate a friend on obtaining it."

In 1826, the United States celebrated its 50th birthday. The people of Quincy asked John Adams to appear at the town's celebration. By this time, he was 90 years old. His health was so bad that he spent his days in bed, and he could not attend the celebration. But he did tell someone what his simple toast would have been. "Independence Forever" was what he wanted to say. In a matter of days, he died—on July 4, 1826, the very day the nation was prepared to celebrate its 50th anniversary.

The nation was filled with sorrow over the loss of one of its founding fathers, a man who dedicated his life to his country. Many people had complained about President Adams while he was in office, but what Americans remembered of him in the end was that he had helped the United States win—and keep—its independence.

Interesting Facts

▶ John Adams and John Quincy Adams were the first father and son to both serve as the U.S. president. It took 175 years for this to happen again. George W. Bush, son of George Bush, became the 43rd president of the United States in 2001. His father was the 41st president.

▶ When John Adams lost his eyesight, his family read books and letters to him. Reading was always one of his passions.

▶ John Adams lived longer than any other president. When he died, he was 90 years and eight months old.

WHEN JOHN ADAMS AND THOMAS JEFFERSON WERE APPOINTED TO THE committee to create the Declaration of Independence, they scarcely knew each other. Adams had seen Jefferson in Congress, but "I never heard him utter three sentences together," he wrote in his autobiography. Still, he knew that Jefferson had the reputation of being a fine writer. Late in life, Adams said the committee wanted him and Jefferson to write the Declaration, but he insisted Jefferson take on the task because he was more popular and a better writer.

In 1784, he and Jefferson worked together after Adams went to Europe to help negotiate business treaties. They remained friends, but they held different views concerning the degree to which Americans could govern themselves. Soon they began to argue. In 1796, Thomas Jefferson was elected John Adams's vice president. They remained at odds. In 1800, Adams was angry and disappointed when he lost the presidential election to Jefferson, and their friendship suffered further. They rekindled their friendship in 1812 through letters, which continued the rest of their days. Amazingly, both John Adams and Thomas Jefferson died on July 4, 1826. Both had been ill but wanted to live until the 50th anniversary of the Declaration of Independence.

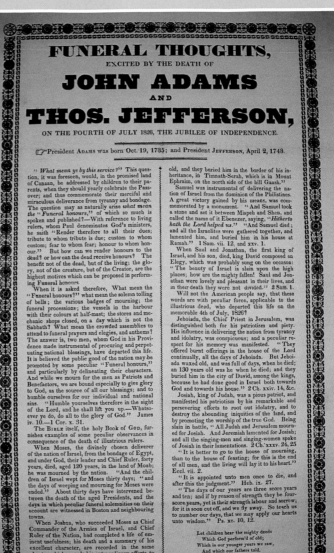

1735 John Adams is born on October 30 in Braintree, Massachusetts. His parents, John Adams and Suzanna Boylston Adams, own a small farm.

1751 Fifteen-year-old John Adams begins taking classes at Harvard College.

1755 Adams graduates from Harvard. He becomes a teacher for a short time to help pay for a law tutor.

1756 Adams starts to study law with a tutor named James Putnam.

1758 Adams opens his own law office. He argues cases all over the Massachusetts colony.

1761 Adams's father dies. He inherits a house and farm in Braintree, where he was born.

1764 Adams marries Abigail Smith. They will have six children, five of whom will live to adulthood.

1765 Adams, now a patriot, believes that England is violating colonists' rights.

1770 Adams is elected to the state legislature. The Boston Massacre takes place in March. Although Adams is committed to American independence, he defends the British soldiers involved in the attack, believing that he must uphold the law.

1773 The Boston Tea Party takes place on December 16.

1774 Adams closes his law office when he is elected to the First Continental Congress. Delegates from all the colonies meet in Philadelphia.

1776 As a member of the Second Continental Congress, Adams is named to the committee asked to write the Declaration of Independence. This will be a statement in which the former colonies say they are no longer part of England.

1777 Congress asks Adams to become a diplomat. He agrees to travel to France and Holland as a representative of the United States.

1779 Adams writes a new constitution for Massachusetts.

1780 As a diplomat, Adams makes arrangements for his country to borrow a large amount of money from Holland.

1783 Adams helps negotiate the Treaty of Paris, officially ending the Revolutionary War.

1784 Abigail Adams joins John Adams in London after years of separations.

1785 Adams becomes the first American diplomat received by the king of England.

1787 A book about constitutions, written by Adams, is published. The Constitutional Convention will use the book to help create the U.S. Constitution.

1788 After more than 10 years of working as a diplomat in Europe, Adams finally returns to the United States.

1789 Adams places second in the first U.S. presidential election, which makes him vice president. George Washington is president.

1793 George Washington and John Adams are both reelected.

1797 John Adams is inaugurated as the second president of the United States. Thomas Jefferson is his vice president. After continued problems between France and the United States, Adams sends U.S. officials to try to improve relations. The French refuse to see the American officials unless they receive money in return. The event is called the XYZ Affair.

1798 The United States begins to fight the French at sea, but the countries never declare war. Congress passes the Alien and Sedition Acts, which are supposed to keep foreigners from making trouble in the United States. The Sedition Act also makes it illegal for Americans to complain in public about the government.

1800 The federal government moves to Washington, D.C. Adams becomes the first president to live in the White House. Diplomats that Adams has sent to France finally negotiate peace. He leaves office after losing the presidential election to Thomas Jefferson and returns to Quincy.

1801 The Alien and Sedition Acts expire.

1812 John Adams writes to his old friend Thomas Jefferson after years of not speaking to him. They renew their friendship, writing many letters to each other for the next 14 years.

1818 John Adams feels great sorrow when Abigail, his wife of 54 years, dies.

1824 John Quincy Adams, son of John and Abigail Adams, is elected president.

July 4, 1826 At nearly 91 years old, John Adams dies on the 50th anniversary of the Declaration of Independence. He lived longer than any other American president that came after. Thomas Jefferson died on the same day, just hours before.

37

alien (AY-lee-un)
An alien is a person who is not a citizen of the country where he or she lives. Congress proposed the Alien Acts to keep the country safe from foreign spies.

bill (BILL)
A bill is an idea for a law presented to a group of lawmakers. Congress and the president decide if bills will become laws.

bribe (BRYB)
A bribe is a reward (such as money) given to people in exchange for their agreeing to do something. French officials refused to see diplomats from the United States unless the Americans paid a bribe.

cabinet (KAB-eh-net)
A cabinet is the group of people who advise a president. John Adams kept the cabinet members that George Washington had chosen.

Constitutional Convention (kon-stih-TOO-shuh-nul kun-VEN-shun)
The Constitutional Convention was the meeting where the U.S. Constitution was written. John Adams's book inspired the men who attended the Constitutional Convention.

constitutions (kon-stih-TOO-shunz)
Constitutions are the set of basic principles that govern a state, country, or society. The U.S. Constitution describes the way the United States is governed.

Continental Congress (kon-tih-NEN-tul KONG-gris)
The Continental Congress was the group of men who governed the United States during and after the Revolution. John Adams was a member of the Continental Congress.

deacon (DEE-kun)
A deacon is a leader of a church. Deacons help ministers run a church.

democracy (deh-MOK-ruh-see)
A democracy is a country in which citizens can vote and help run the government. The United States is a democracy.

diplomat (DIP-luh-mat)
A diplomat is a government official whose job is to represent a country in discussions with other countries. John Adams was a diplomat.

Glossary TERMS

**electoral college
(ee-LEKT-uh-rul KOL-ij)**
The electoral college is made up of representatives from each state who vote for candidates in presidential elections. Members of the electoral college cast their votes based on which candidate most people in their state prefer.

federal (FED-ur-ul)
Federal means having to do with the central government of the United States, rather than a state or city government. Federalists believed that the U.S. federal government should have control over the states.

**Federalist Party
(FED-ur-ul-ist PAR-tee)**
The Federalist Party was a political party in Adams's time. Federalists believed that a few well-educated people should run the nation.

foreign affairs (FOR-un uh-FAIRZ)
Foreign affairs are matters involving other (foreign) countries. The president has to deal with foreign affairs, as well as problems at home.

immigrants (IM-uh-grentz)
Immigrants are people who move from their homeland to a new country. Part of the Alien and Sedition Acts increased the length of time it took for immigrants to become U.S. citizens.

**inauguration
(ih-naw-gyuh-RAY-shun)**
An inauguration is the ceremony that takes place when a new president begins a term. John Adams administered the oath of office to George Washington at Washington's inauguration.

influenced (IN-floo-enst)
If someone can be influenced, others can convince him or her to think a certain way. John Adams was not easily influenced by other people's opinions.

inheritance (in-HAIR-uh-tents)
An inheritance is something one person leaves to another when he or she dies. John Adams received an inheritance from his father.

legislature (LEJ-uh-slay-chur)
A legislature is a group of people elected to make laws. John Adams was elected to the Massachusetts legislature.

Glossary TERMS

monarchy (MON-arr-kee)
A monarchy is a government run by a monarch, such as a king or a queen. Great Britain is a monarchy.

negotiate (nee-GOH-she-ayt)
If people negotiate, they talk things over and try to come to an agreement. John Adams helped negotiate a treaty between the United States and England.

neutral (NOO-trul)
If a country is neutral, it does not take sides during a war. George Washington believed the United States should remain neutral, rather than take sides in European wars.

nominate (NOM-uh-nayt)
If a political party nominates someone, it chooses him or her to run for a political office. The Federalist Party nominated John Adams as its presidential candidate.

officials (uh-FISH-ulz)
Officials are people who hold important positions, often in the government. English officials collected taxes from American colonists.

policies (PAWL-uh-seez)
Policies are rules made to help run a government or other organization. The founding fathers created policies for the new country.

political parties (poh-LIT-uh-kul PAR-teez)
Political parties are groups of people who share similar ideas about how to run a government. Today the two major U.S. political parties are the Democratic and Republican parties.

politics (PAWL-uh-tiks)
Politics refers to the actions and practices of the government. As a young man, John Adams wrote about politics.

preside (preh-ZYD)
If someone presides over a meeting, he or she is in charge of it and must keep order during discussions. Vice President Adams presided over the Senate.

representatives (rep-ree-ZEN-tuh-tivz)
Representatives are people who attend a meeting, having agreed to speak or act for others. Congress is made up of representatives elected by the American people.

Republican Party
(ree-PUB-luh-ken PAR-tee)
The Republican Party was a political party in John Adams's time. The Republican Party was also known as the Democratic-Republican Party.

revolution (rev-uh-LOO-shun)
A revolution is something that causes a complete change in government. The American Revolution was a war fought between the United States and England.

sedition (suh-DIH-shun)
Sedition is something said or written, such as a newspaper article, that causes people to rebel against their government. American officials feared sedition during John Adams's presidency.

spokesperson (SPOHKS-pur-son)
A spokesperson is one person who speaks for a group. Adams became a spokesperson for the patriots.

surrender (suh-REN-dur)
If an army surrenders, it gives up to the enemy. When British General Cornwallis surrendered, he promised his soldiers would no longer fight the Americans.

treaty (TREE-tee)
A treaty is a formal agreement made between nations. The United States and England signed a peace treaty after the American Revolution ended.

tutor (TOO-tur)
To tutor is to give private lessons to someone. A lawyer agreed to tutor John Adams so he could learn about law.

Our Presidents

President	Birthplace	Life Span	Presidency	Political Party	First Lady
George Washington	Virginia	1732–1799	1789–1797	None	Martha Dandridge Custis Washington
John Adams	Massachusetts	1735–1826	1797–1801	Federalist	Abigail Smith Adams
Thomas Jefferson	Virginia	1743–1826	1801–1809	Democratic-Republican	widower
James Madison	Virginia	1751–1836	1809–1817	Democratic Republican	Dolley Payne Todd Madison
James Monroe	Virginia	1758–1831	1817–1825	Democratic Republican	Elizabeth Kortright Monroe
John Quincy Adams	Massachusetts	1767–1848	1825–1829	Democratic-Republican	Louisa Johnson Adams
Andrew Jackson	South Carolina	1767–1845	1829–1837	Democrat	widower
Martin Van Buren	New York	1782–1862	1837–1841	Democrat	widower
William H. Harrison	Virginia	1773–1841	1841	Whig	Anna Symmes Harrison
John Tyler	Virginia	1790–1862	1841–1845	Whig	Letitia Christian Tyler / Julia Gardiner Tyler
James K. Polk	North Carolina	1795–1849	1845–1849	Democrat	Sarah Childress Polk

42

Our PRESIDENTS

President	Birthplace	Life Span	Presidency	Political Party	First Lady
Zachary Taylor	Virginia	1784–1850	1849–1850	Whig	Margaret Mackall Smith Taylor
Millard Fillmore	New York	1800–1874	1850–1853	Whig	Abigail Powers Fillmore
Franklin Pierce	New Hampshire	1804–1869	1853–1857	Democrat	Jane Means Appleton Pierce
James Buchanan	Pennsylvania	1791–1868	1857–1861	Democrat	never married
Abraham Lincoln	Kentucky	1809–1865	1861–1865	Republican	Mary Todd Lincoln
Andrew Johnson	North Carolina	1808–1875	1865–1869	Democrat	Eliza McCardle Johnson
Ulysses S. Grant	Ohio	1822–1885	1869–1877	Republican	Julia Dent Grant
Rutherford B. Hayes	Ohio	1822–1893	1877–1881	Republican	Lucy Webb Hayes
James A. Garfield	Ohio	1831–1881	1881	Republican	Lucretia Rudolph Garfield
Chester A. Arthur	Vermont	1829–1886	1881–1885	Republican	widower
Grover Cleveland	New Jersey	1837–1908	1885–1889	Democrat	Frances Folsom Cleveland

Our PRESIDENTS

President	Birthplace	Life Span	Presidency	Political Party	First Lady
Benjamin Harrison	Ohio	1833–1901	1889–1893	Republican	Caroline Scott Harrison
Grover Cleveland	New Jersey	1837–1908	1893–1897	Democrat	Frances Folsom Cleveland
William McKinley	Ohio	1843–1901	1897–1901	Republican	Ida Saxton McKinley
Theodore Roosevelt	New York	1858–1919	1901–1909	Republican	Edith Kermit Carow Roosevelt
William H. Taft	Ohio	1857–1930	1909–1913	Republican	Helen Herron Taft
Woodrow Wilson	Virginia	1856–1924	1913–1921	Democrat	Ellen L. Axson Wilson Edith Bolling Galt Wilson
Warren G. Harding	Ohio	1865–1923	1921–1923	Republican	Florence Kling De Wolfe Harding
Calvin Coolidge	Vermont	1872–1933	1923–1929	Republican	Grace Goodhue Coolidge
Herbert C. Hoover	Iowa	1874–1964	1929–1933	Republican	Lou Henry Hoover
Franklin D. Roosevelt	New York	1882–1945	1933–1945	Democrat	Anna Eleanor Roosevelt Roosevelt
Harry S. Truman	Missouri	1884–1972	1945–1953	Democrat	Elizabeth Wallace Truman

Our PRESIDENTS

President	Birthplace	Life Span	Presidency	Political Party	First Lady
Dwight D. Eisenhower	Texas	1890–1969	1953–1961	Republican	Mary "Mamie" Doud Eisenhower
John F. Kennedy	Massachusetts	1917–1963	1961–1963	Democrat	Jacqueline Bouvier Kennedy
Lyndon B. Johnson	Texas	1908–1973	1963–1969	Democrat	Claudia Alta Taylor Johnson
Richard M. Nixon	California	1913–1994	1969–1974	Republican	Thelma Catherine Ryan Nixon
Gerald Ford	Nebraska	1913–	1974–1977	Republican	Elizabeth "Betty" Bloomer Warren Ford
James Carter	Georgia	1924–	1977–1981	Democrat	Rosalynn Smith Carter
Ronald Reagan	Illinois	1911–	1981–1989	Republican	Nancy Davis Reagan
George Bush	Massachusetts	1924–	1989–1993	Republican	Barbara Pierce Bush
William Clinton	Arkansas	1946–	1993–2001	Democrat	Hillary Rodham Clinton
George W. Bush	Connecticut	1946–	2001–	Republican	Laura Welch Bush

Presidential FACTS

Qualifications
To run for president, a candidate must
- be at least 35 years old
- be a citizen who was born in the United States
- have lived in the United States for 14 years

Term of Office
A president's term of office is four years. No president can stay in office for more than two terms.

Election Date
The presidential election takes place every four years on the first Tuesday of November.

Inauguration Date
Presidents are inaugurated on January 20.

Oath of Office
I do solemnly swear I will faithfully execute the office of the President of the United States and will to the best of my ability preserve, protect, and defend the Constitution of the United States.

Write a Letter to the President
One of the best things about being a U.S. citizen is that Americans get to participate in their government. They can speak out if they feel government leaders aren't doing their jobs. They can also praise leaders who are going the extra mile. Do you have something you'd like the president to do? Should the president worry more about the environment and encourage people to recycle? Should the government spend more money on our schools? You can write a letter to the president to say how you feel!

1600 Pennsylvania Avenue
Washington, D.C. 20500

You can even send an e-mail to: president@whitehouse.gov

For Further INFORMATION

Internet Sites

Learn more about John Adams:
http://www.whitehouse.gov/WH/glimpse/presidents/html/ja2.html
http://www.webcom.com:80/bba/ch/adams/abio.html
http://www.potus.com/jadams.html
http://www.masshist.org/html/adams_papers.html

Learn more about Abigail Adams:
http://nimbus.ocis.temple.edu/~rkarras/kgraham.htm

Visit the Adams National Historical Site:
http://www.nps.gov/adam/

See Quincy, Massachusetts, and its many historic sites:
http://www.quincyonline.com

Find out more about the Declaration of Independence:
http://www.lcweb2.loc.gov/const/abt_declar.html

Tour the White House:
http://www.whitehouse.gov/WH/glimpse/tour.html

Learn more about all the presidents and visit the White House:
http://www.whitehouse.gov/WH/glimpse/presidents/html/presidents.html
http://www.thepresidency.org/presinfo.htm
http://www.americanpresidents.org

Books

Debman, Betty. *A Kid's Guide to the White House.* Kansas City, MO: Andrews McMeel, 1997.

Feinberg, Barbara Silberdick. *Next in Line: The American Vice Presidency.* New York: Franklin Watts, 1996.

Hering, Marianne. *Secret of the Missing Teacup* (White House Adventure series). Colorado Springs, CO: Chariot Victor, 1998.

Rubel, David. *Scholastic Encyclopedia of the Presidents and Their Times.* New York: Scholastic, 1994.

Wagoner, Jean Brown. *Abigail Adams: Girl of Colonial Days.* New York: Aladdin, 1992.

Index